Avgusta Udartseva

25 Most Popular Classical Pieces *for Piano*

Beethoven, Bach, Mozart, Debussy, Handel / Halvorsen, Rachmaninoff and Many More!
With Online Audio

ISBN: 978-1-962612-16-6

Assistant Anastasia Skvorets

The piano on the cover - © PantherMediaSeller / depositphotos

Messages about typos, errors, inaccuracies and suggestions for improving the quality are gratefully received at:
avgustaudartseva@gmail.com

CONTENTS

1. Für Elise

Bagatelle No. 25, WoO 59

Ludwig van Beethoven

Poco moto

31
35
40
Ped.
46
52

Ped.
Ped.
pp
8va

84
Ped.
89
95
100

2. «Air»

Orchestral Suite No. 3 in D Major, Movement II
BWV 1068

Johann Sebastian Bach

Adagio ♩ = 60

mp

dim.

poco a poco cresc.

3. Moonlight Sonata

Op. 27, No. 2, First Movement

Ludwig van Beethoven

Adagio sostenuto

sempre pianissimo e senza sordino

pp

cresc.
decresc.

28
p
31
34
37
40
decresc.
pp
pp

58
cresc.
p
pp
61
64
decresc.
67
pp
attacca subito il sequente

4. Waltz

Op. 39, No. 8, from Children's Album

Pyotr Ilyich Tchaikovsky

Presto

dim.

Waltz

5. Toccata in D Minor

BWV 565

Johann Sebastian Bach

Adagio molto ♩ = 60

R.h.

L.h.

ff

R.h.

Ped.

Ped.

Allegro

mf

cresc.

allargando
mf
f
p
8va

a tempo
allargando
a tempo
mf
f
allargando
a tempo
mf
f
Ped.

47
Allegro moderato
50
cresc.
53
56
Molto maestoso
pesante
simile
rit.
8va

6. Adagio in G Minor

Music: Tomaso Albinoni
arr. by Avgusta Udartseva, Anastasia Skvorets

Adagio

p *dolce e poco stacc.*

simile

dolce ma pieno

simile

17
20
p
poco fraseggiando
23
simile
26

7. *Adagio*

Concert for harpsichord No. 3, Second Movement
BWV 974

Johann Sebastian Bach

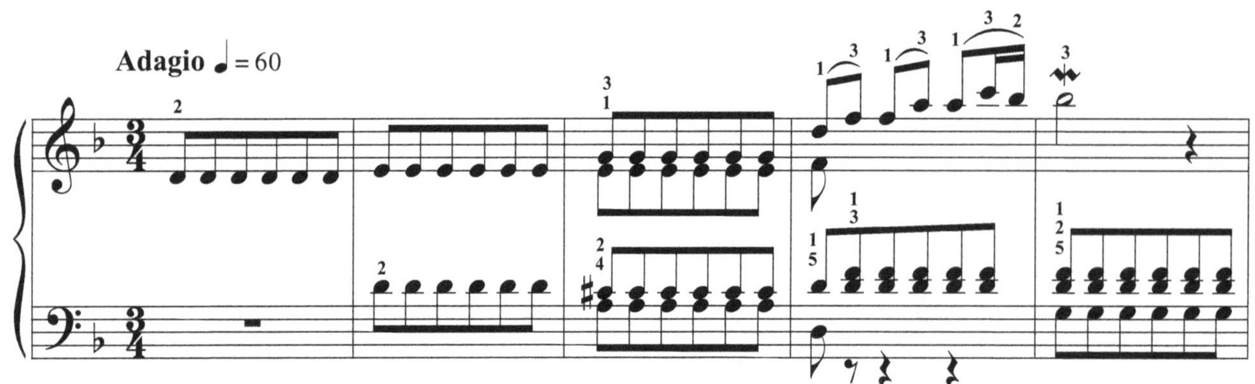

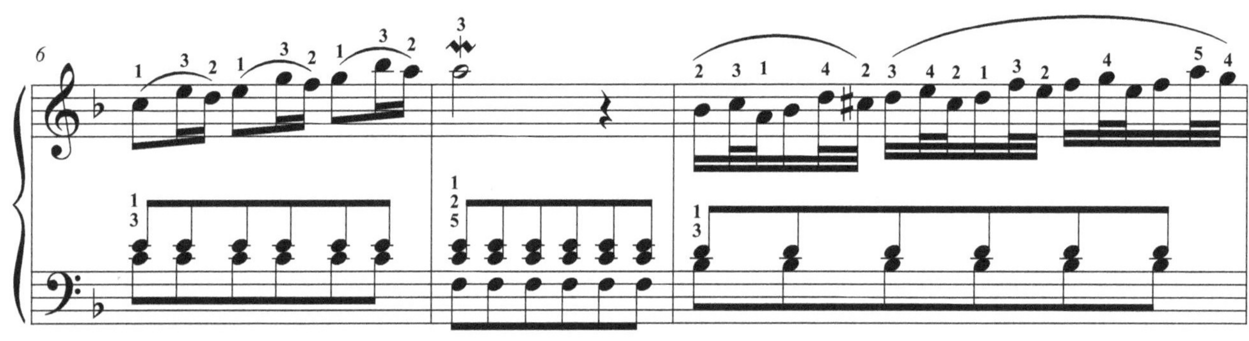

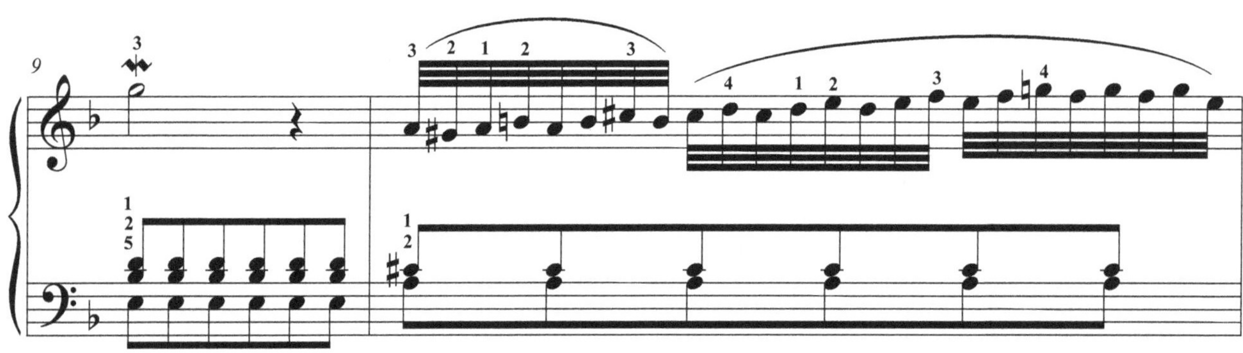

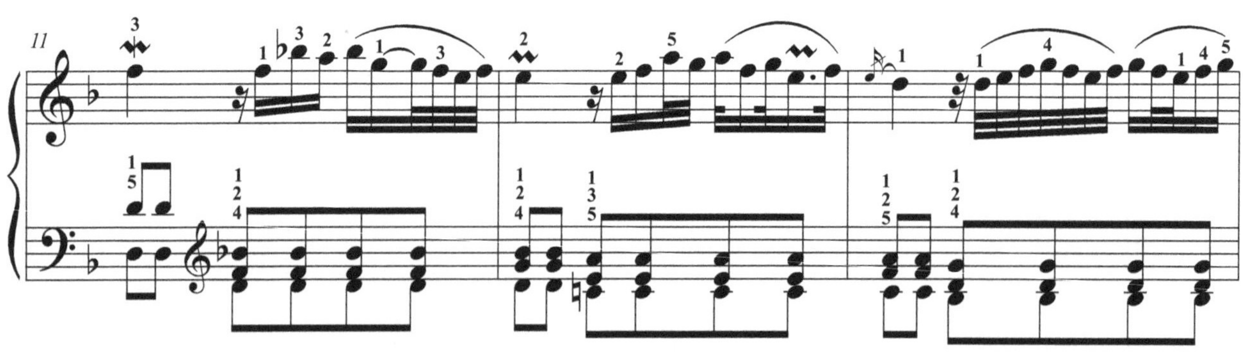

Adagio

Adagio

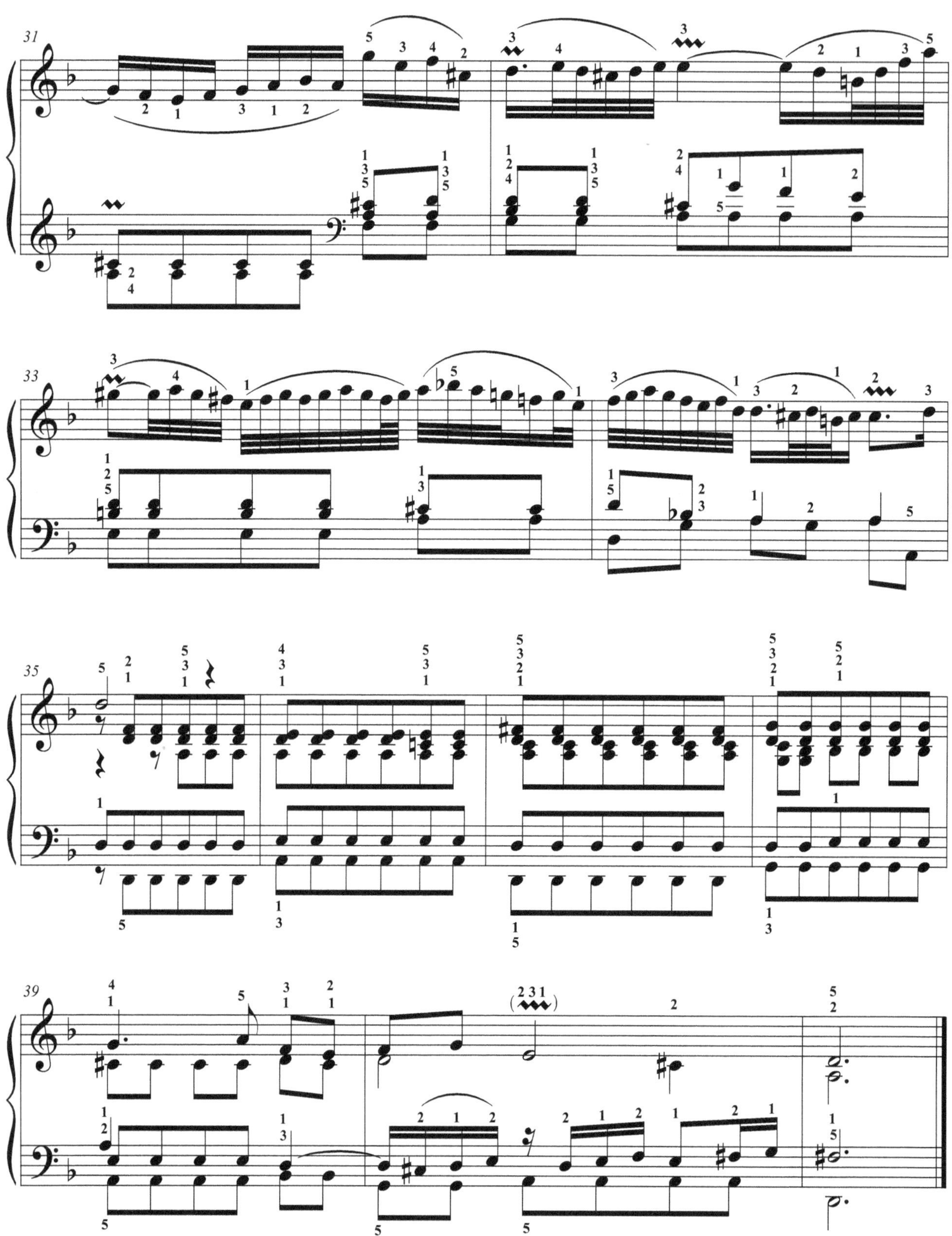

8. Symphony No. 40 in G Minor

K. 550, First Movement

Music: Wolfgang Amadeus Mozart
arr. by Anastasia Skvorets

Allegro molto

f
sf

p

63
f
sf
69
p
sf
73
f
76
p

80
88
92
96
f
f
sf

9. Sarabande

from the Suite for harpsichord Vol. 2 No 4 d-moll,
HWV 437

George Frideric Handel

Grave

mf non legato

p sempre legato

Sarabande

10. Nocturne in C-sharp Minor

No. 20, B. 49

Frédéric Chopin

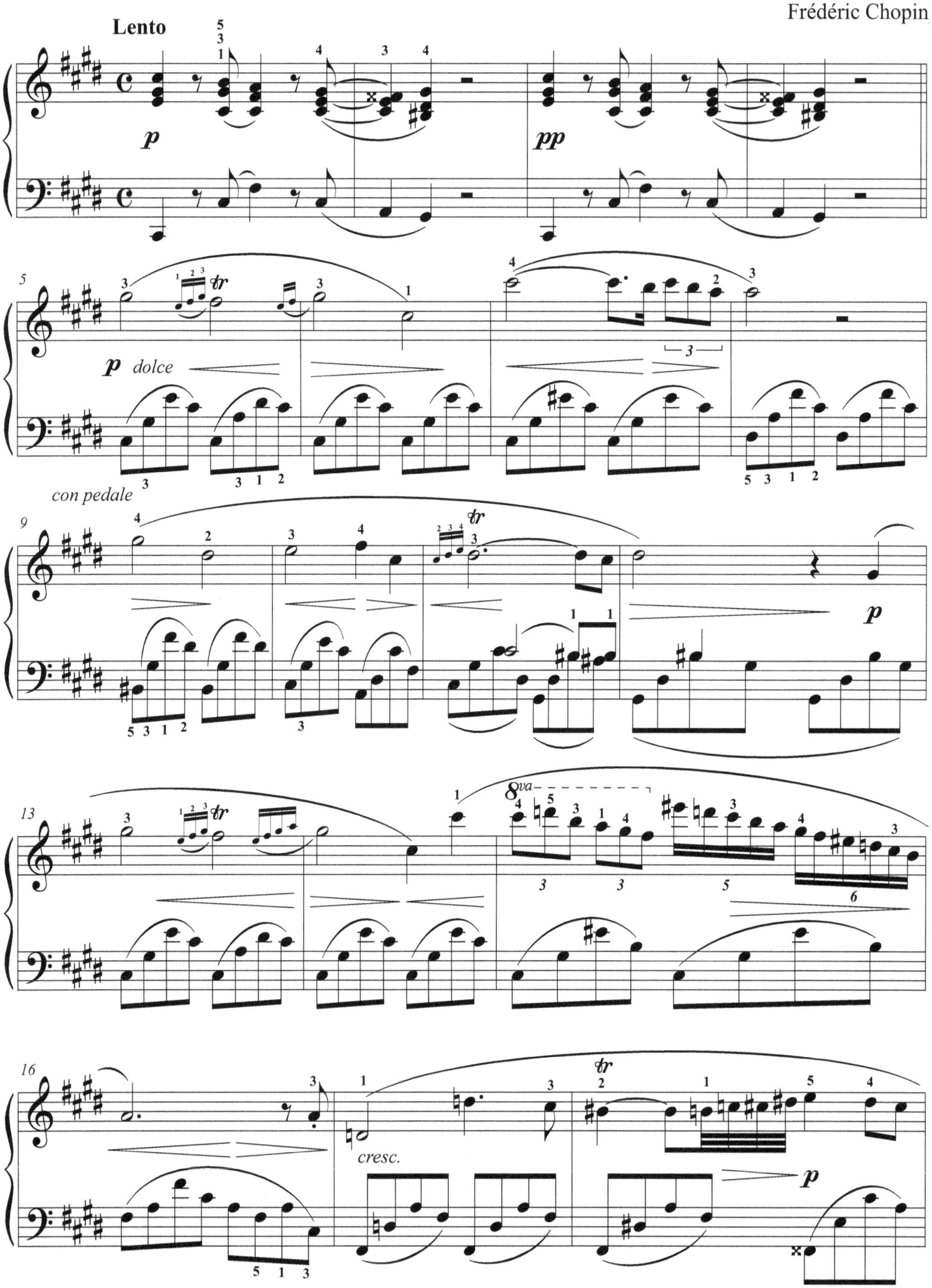

Lento

p

pp

p dolce

con pedale

cresc.

pp
mf
pp
mf
p
pp
p
dim.
f
dim.
p

mp
sempre più piano rallentando
Adagio
rit.
ppp
p
Tempo I
dolce
8va
f
p
f
p
pp

59
8va
35
11
61
13
pp
63
pp

11. Gymnopédie

No. 1, ES 10

Erik Satie

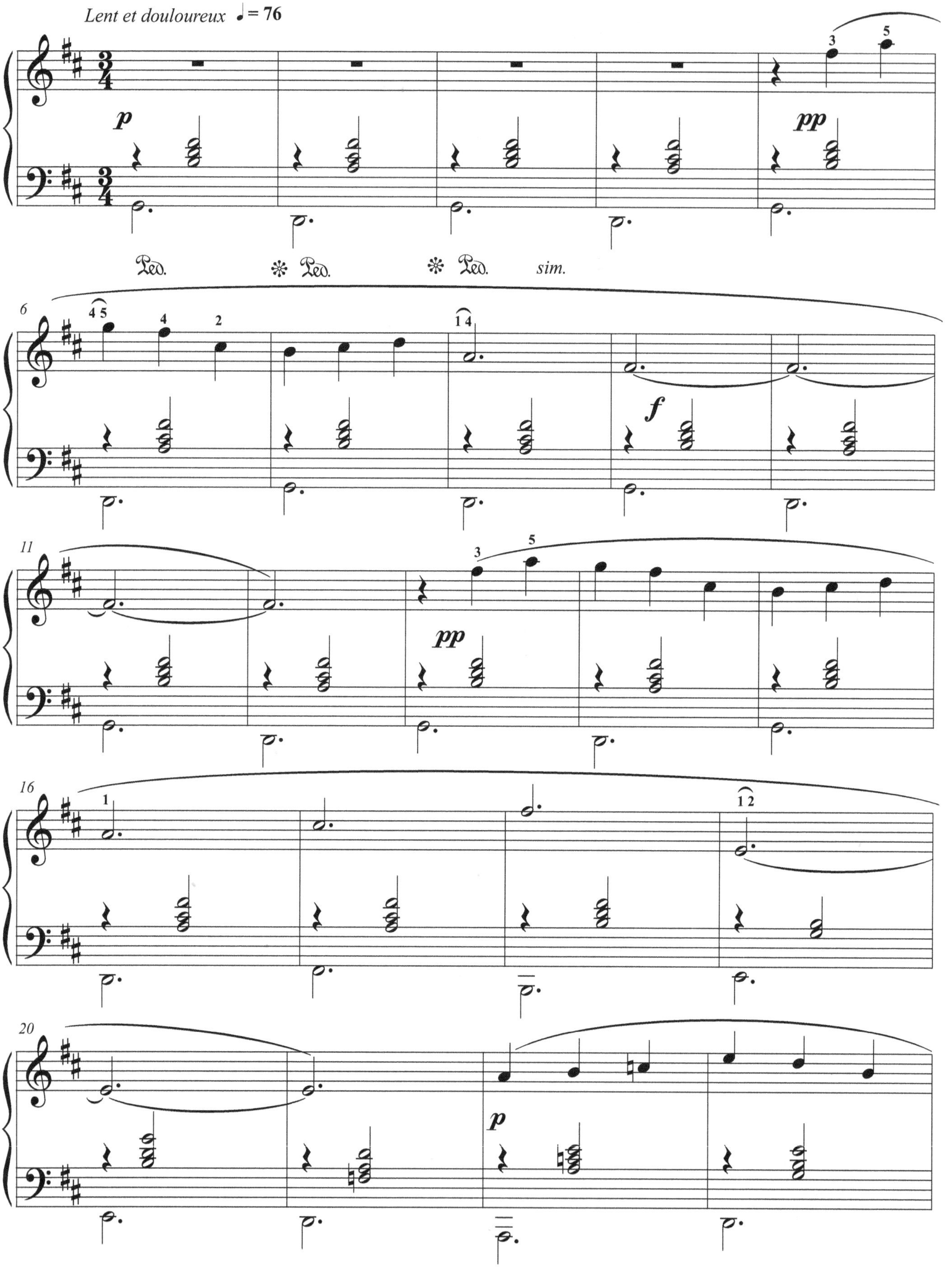

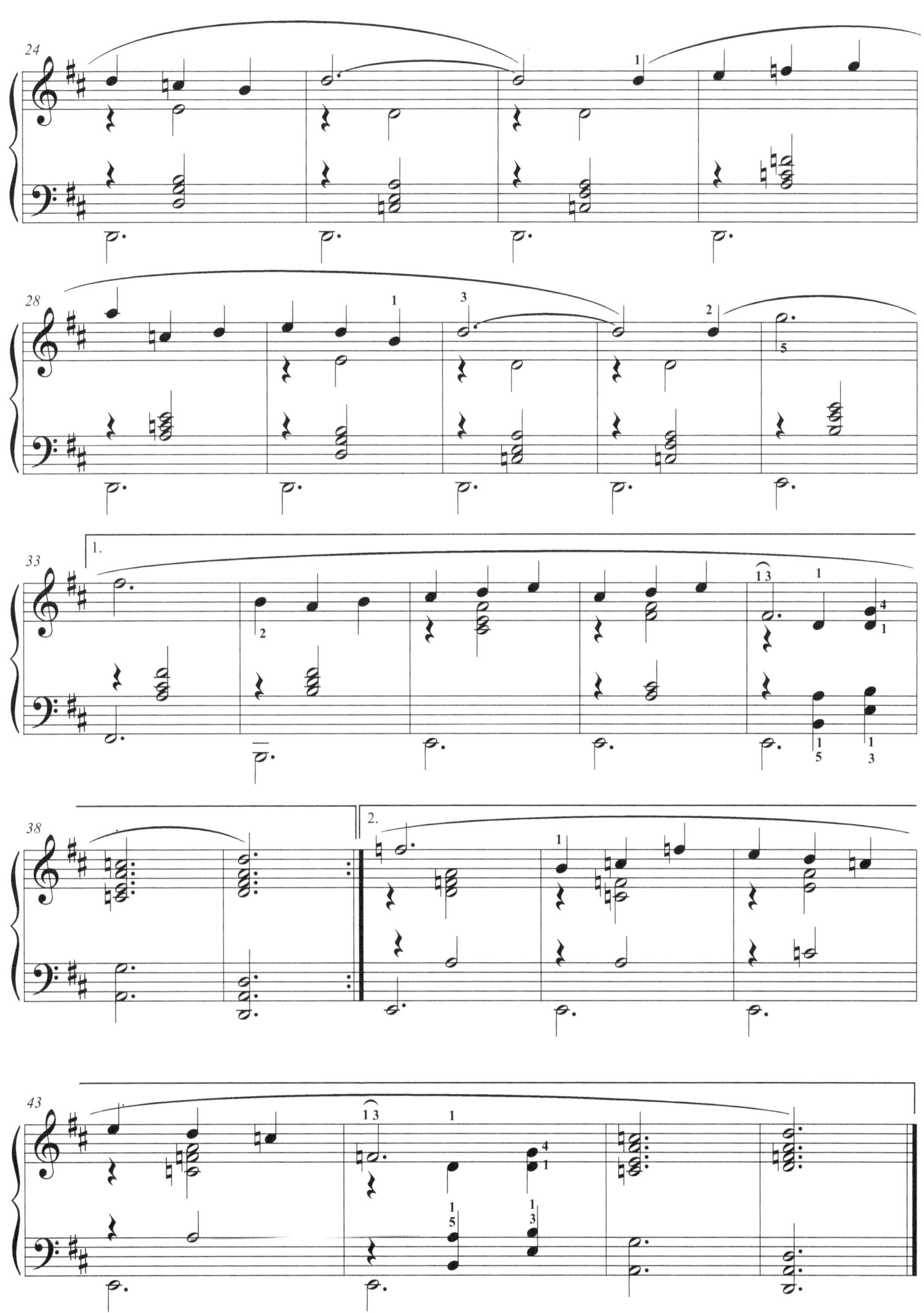
24
28
33
1.
38
2.
43

12. Arabesque

L. 66, No. 1

Claude Debussy

Andantino con moto

p

Ped. ❊ Ped. ❊ Ped. ❊

4

rit.

a tempo

pp

Ped. ❊ Ped. ❊ Ped. ❊

7

Ped. ❊ Ped. ❊ Ped. ❊

10

stringendo

poco a poco cresc.

sempre cresc.

Ped. ❊ Ped. ❊ Ped. ❊ Ped. ❊

14
rit.
Ped.
17
p
20
rit.
p
23
a tempo
rit.
p
a tempo
p
Poco mosso
cresc.

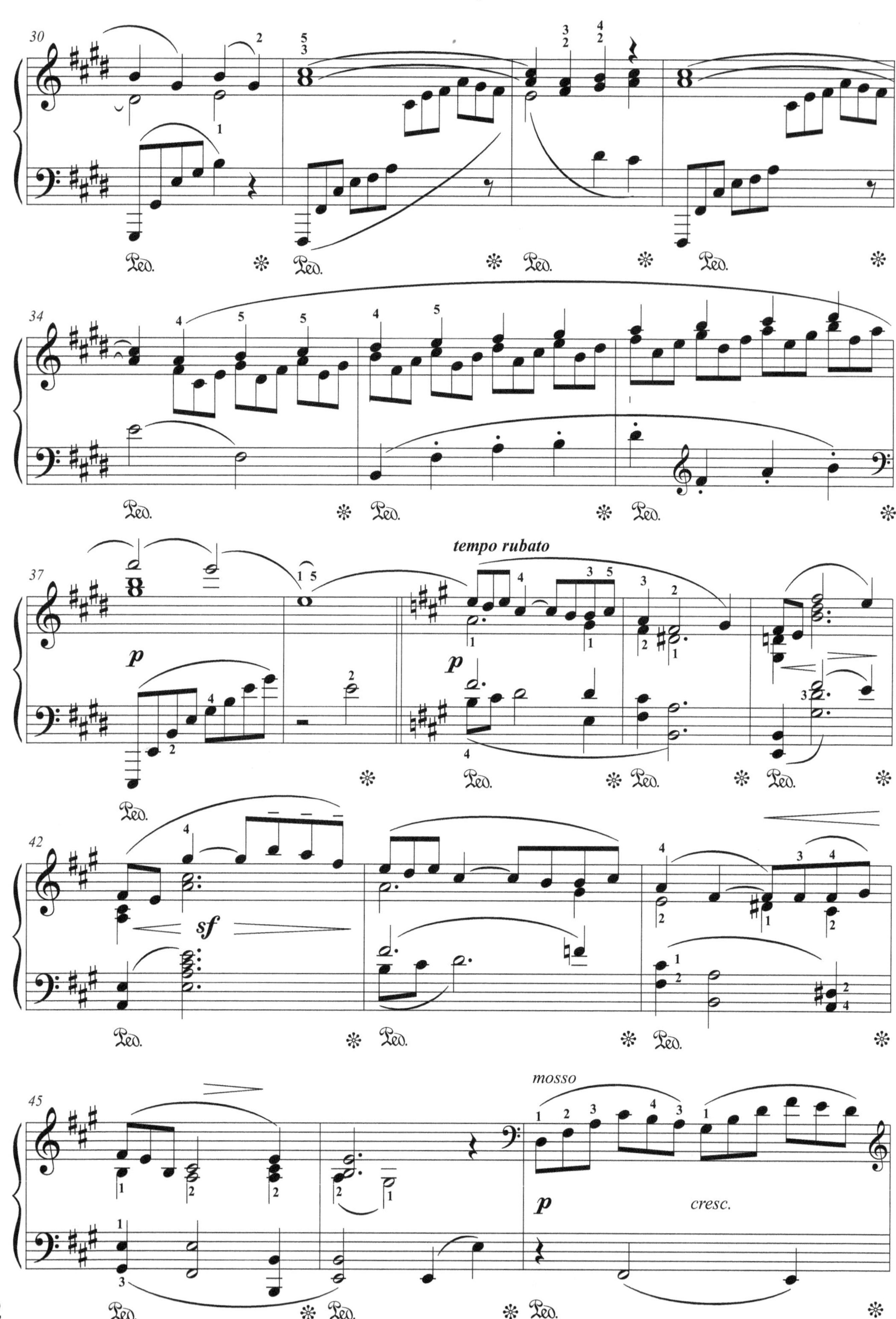
tempo rubato
p
p
sf
mosso
p
cresc.

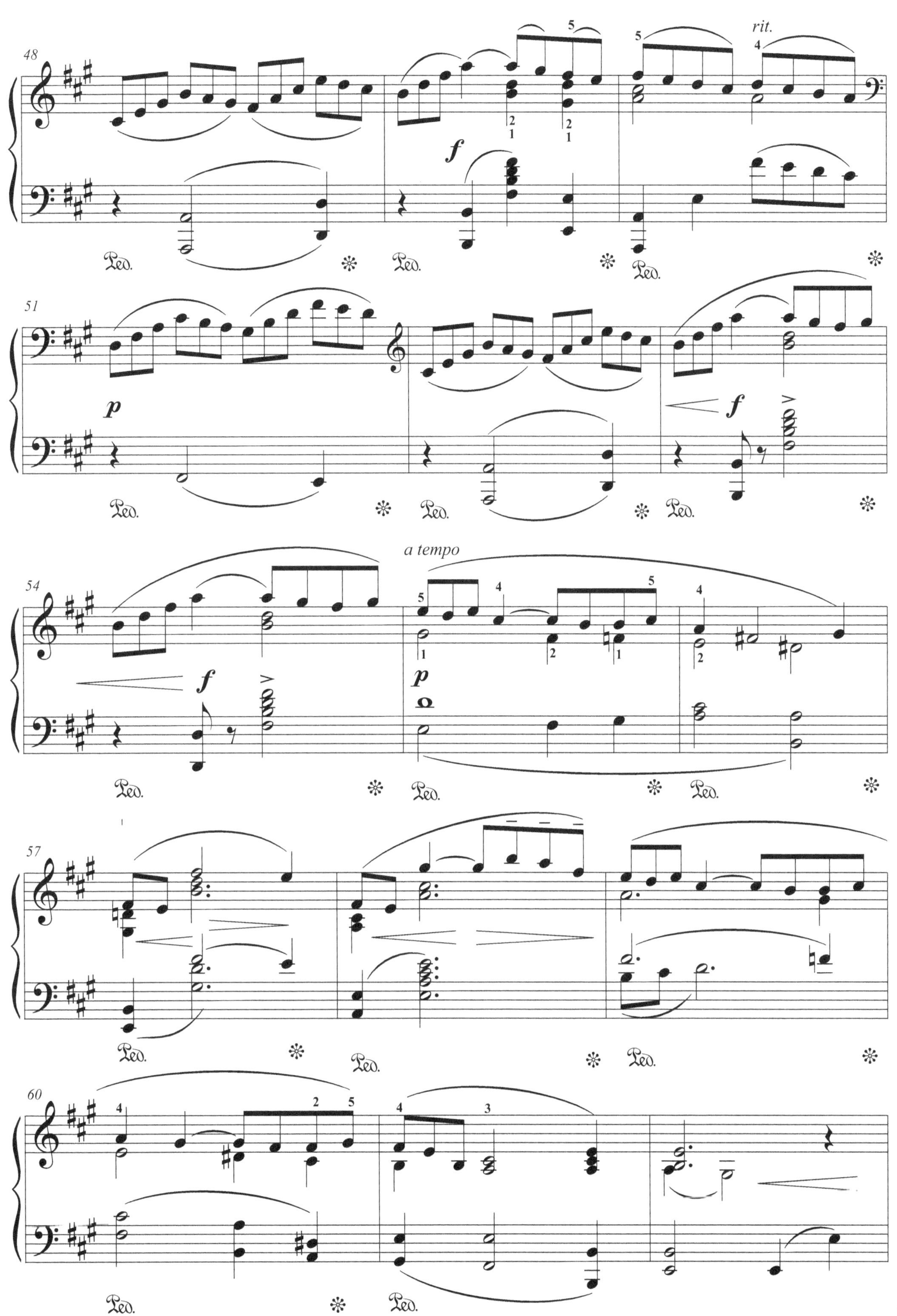
rit.
a tempo
Ped.

63
risoluto
f
Ped.
67
rit.
dim. molto
più dim.
Ped.
Tempo I
71
p
Ped.
74
rit.
a tempo
pp
Ped.

poco a poco cresc.
stringendo
sempre cresc.
rit.
a tempo
p

91
Ped.
93
Ped.
95
dim.
Ped.
97
dim.
Ped.
99
p
Ped.

101
pp
3
3
3
3
Ped.
Ped.
103
3
3
3
3
3
3
3
3
Ped.
Ped.
105
3
3
3
3
pp
Ped.
Ped.

13. Passacaglia

G. F. Handel / J. Halvorsen
arr. by Avgusta Udartseva

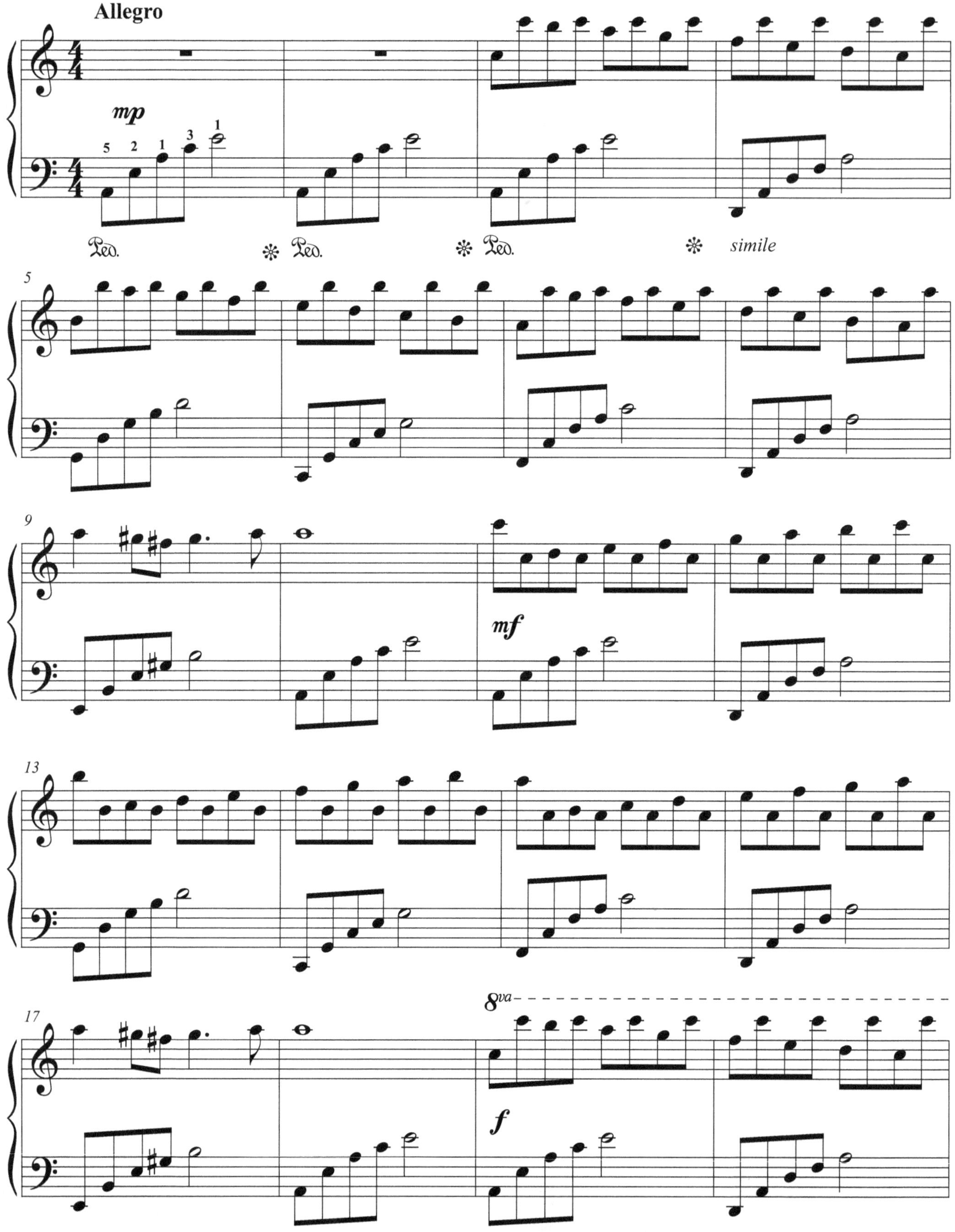

Allegro

mp

Ped. * Ped. * Ped. * *simile*

mf

f

8va

(8va)
21
8va
25
29
33
37

Passacaglia

61
65
mp
69
72
p

Original Piece - 13. Passacaglia

G. F. Handel / J. Halvorsen

Allegro

mp

Ped. * Ped. *

simile

5

9

13

17

21
25
29
33
37

41
45
49
53
57

14. Prelude in E Minor

Op. 28, No. 4

Frédéric Chopin

Largo

p *espress.*

stretto

f

dim.

19
p
22
pp

15. Prelude

Op. 23, No. 5

Sergei Rachmaninoff

Alla marcia ♩ = 108

cresc.

4

f

dim.

7

p

dim.

pp

10

p

cresc.

13
f
marcato
17
f
20
f
23
ff
p
25
ff

28
31
dim.
34
Un poco meno mosso
p
dim.
pp
36

38
cresc.
40
mf
p
42
m.d.
44
m.d.

46
cresc.
mf
48
p
rit.
dim.
(♭)
poco a poco accelerando
50
ppp
53
al tempo I
56
Tempo I
f

59
cresc.
62
ff
f
65
68
f
70
ff
p

72
ff
75
78
dim.
81
p
dim.
84
pp leggiero

16. Fantasia in D minor

K. 397

Wolfgang Amadeus Mozart

Andante

p

Adagio

p

cresc.
cresc.
cresc.

Presto
L.H.
L.H.
Tempo I
f
p
cresc.
f
p
cresc.
f

Allegretto
dolce

66
72
1.
2.
77
82
86
90

rall.
a tempo
f
p
f
p
pp
f
ff

17. Minuet in G Major

BWV Anh. 116

Johann Sebastian Bach

Andante ♩ = 120

f *p* *cresc.* *f* *p* *p*

cresc.
f
p
cresc.
f
p
f

18. Sonatina

Op. 36, No. 1

Muzio Clementi

Spiritoso ♩ = 120

Sonatina

Sonatina

Sonatina

Sonatina

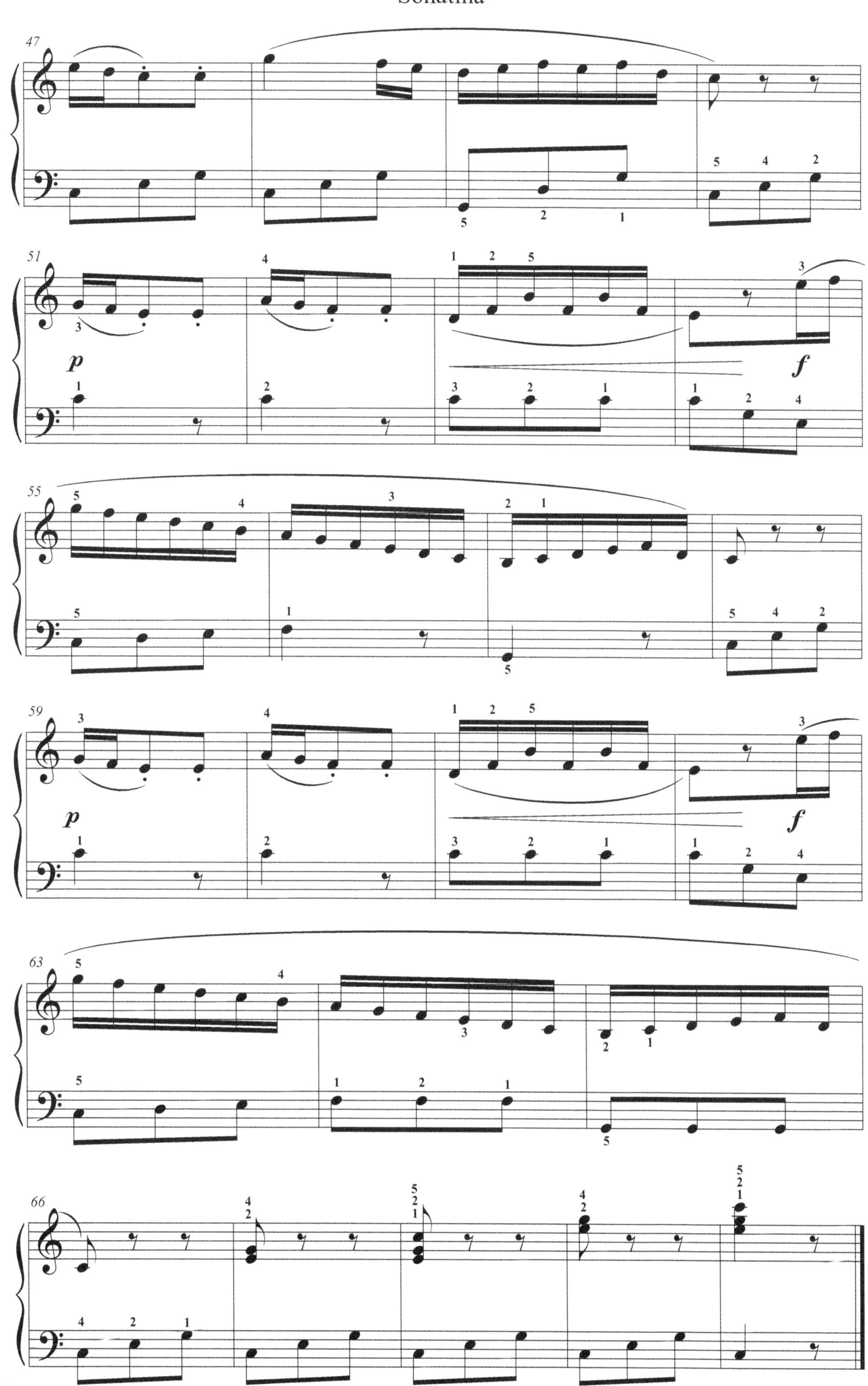

19. Minuet in G Major

WoO 10, No. 2

Ludwig van Beethoven

Fine

Trio

D.C. al Fine

20. Les Sauvages

RCT 6:7, No. 14

Jean-Philippe Rameau

Allegro ♩ = 120

legato

legato

fine

legato
legato

da capo al fine

21. Träumerei

Op. 15, No. 7, Scenes from Childhood

Robert Schumann

♩ = 100

p

5

ritardando

9

13

ritardando

17
21
ritardando
p

22. Moment Musical

Op. 94, No. 3

Franz Schubert

Allegro moderato

29
p
34
39
ppp
dim.
44
dim.
49

23. Les Cyclopes

RCT 3:8, No. 17

Jean-Philippe Rameau

Allegro 𝅗𝅥 = 100

legato
legato

44
48
51
tr

24. Sonatina in G Major

Anh. 5, First and Second Movement

Ludwig van Beethoven

Moderato

Romanze

poco rit.
a tempo
mf
p
mf
p

25. Siciliano

From Flute Sonata BWV 1031

Johann Sebastian Bach
arr. by Eugène d'Albert

Andantino ♩ = 80

p mf mf mf p mf

con Pedale

18
p
mf
p
21
mf
p
mf
25
29
mf
rall.
p

Audio Links

All of the audio files are also available on Google Drive:

or use the link:

cutt.ly/PeVxn6TJ

Important! Be sure to download all files from Google Drive to your computer. We did have a glitch in our system once and our files were temporarily unavailable online. It would be best to download them all at once so you have offline access to them anytime.

Some videos are also available on YouTube:

or use the link:

cutt.ly/QwvuOxc0

For any questions, comments or suggestions, email us at:
avgustaudartseva@gmail.com

Easy Saxophone for Beginners: Theory, Practice and 55 Songs. For Kids 12+ and Adults. With Online Video and Audio

Complete saxophone instruction book for beginners. For kids 12+ and adults.

This step-by-step guide is for anyone who wants to master the instrument and learn to play their favorite songs effortlessly. The book is also for those who want to learn to swing, play the blues and practice improvisation.

ISBN: 978-1962612098

ASIN: 1962612090

United States | United Kingdom | Canada

Easy Recorder Lessons for Kids + Video and Audio: Beginner Recorder for Children and Teens with 60 Songs. First Book Step by Step

- Learn the position of the body and hands, how to breathe properly and play easily;
- Letters above each note and simple explanations;
- Convenient large US Letter print size;
- Video accompaniment to all lessons by direct link inside the book;
- 2-in-1 Book: Recorder lessons and video + 60 Songs.

ISBN: 979-8386419004

ASIN: B0BXMX7ZVN

United States | United Kingdom | Canada

And it's great for adults

www.ingramcontent.com/pod-product-compliance
Lightning Source LLC
Chambersburg PA
CBHW081516040426
42447CB00013B/3244

* 9 7 8 1 9 6 2 6 1 2 1 6 6 *